For my family,
and for Lou

Text copyright © 2014 by Diane E. Muldrow
Cover photograph © Mary Evans/Classic Stock/H. Armstrong Roberts
All rights reserved.
Published in the United States by Golden Books, an imprint of Random House Children's Books, a division
of Random House LLC, 1745 Broadway, New York, NY 10019, and in Canada by Random House of Canada
Limited, Toronto, Penguin Random House Companies. Golden Books, A Golden Book, A Little Golden Book,
the G colophon, and the distinctive gold spine are registered trademarks of Random House LLC.
The Poky Little Puppy, The Little Red Hen, The Saggy Baggy Elephant, Scuffy the Tugboat,
Tawny Scrawny Lion, and Tootle are registered trademarks of Random House LLC.
The artwork contained in this work was previously published in separate works by Golden Books, New York.
Copyright © 1942–2014 by Random House LLC.

Artwork on copyright page, title page, and page 93 from *The Little Golden Holiday Book* by Marion Conger,
illustrated by Eloise Wilkin, copyright © 1951, renewed 1979 by Random House LLC.

randomhousekids.com
dianemuldrow.com
Library of Congress Control Number: 2014939060

ISBN 978-0-553-50875-8 (trade) — ISBN 978-0-375-97414-4 (lib. bdg.) — ISBN 978-0-553-50876-5 (ebook)
PRINTED IN CHINA
10 9 8 7 6 5 4 3 2 1
Random House Children's Books supports the First Amendment and celebrates the right to read.

Everything I Need to Know About LOVE I Learned From a Little Golden Book

DIANE MULDROW

𝓰 A GOLDEN BOOK • NEW YORK

From *Tootle* by Gertrude Crampton, illustrated by Tibor Gergely, 1945.

Is your love life going off the tracks?

Always the bridesmaid,

never the bride?

From *The Paper Doll Wedding* by Hilda Miloche and Wilma Kane, 1954.

Perhaps you wonder if
you'll ever find true love.

From *The Little Golden Book of Poetry*, illustrated by Corinne Malvern, 1947.

**Without love in your heart,
life can feel so tedious,**

From *The House That Jack Built*, illustrated by J. P. Miller, 1954.

so routine.

From *Daddies* by Janet Frank, illustrated by Tibor Gergely, 1953.

**You feel like a castaway,
a stranger in a strange land.**

From *The Sailor Dog* by Margaret Wise Brown, illustrated by Garth Williams, 1953.

Perhaps you've been looking for love
in all the wrong places?

From *The Musicians of Bremen*, adapted from the Brothers Grimm, illustrated by J. P. Miller, 1954.

Remember that everyone feels lonely now and then.

From *Little Gray Donkey* by Alice Lunt, illustrated by Tibor Gergely, 1954.

Don't be discouraged. . . .

New friends may be just around the corner!

From *The Happy Man and His Dump Truck* by Miryam, illustrated by Tibor Gergely, 1950.

One day a handsome stranger
may appear out of nowhere.

From *The Wild Swans* by Hans Christian Andersen, illustrated by Gordon Laite, 1970, 2014.

He's got you under a spell!

From *The Seven Sneezes* by Olga Cabral, illustrated by Tibor Gergely, 1948.

But don't get so carried away

From "Toads and Diamonds,"
The Blue Book of Fairy Tales,
illustrated by Gordon Laite, 1959.

that you neglect your friends.

From *Robert and His New Friends* by Nina Schneider, illustrated by Corinne Malvern, 1951.

Of course, there are a lot of wolves out there.

They do *not* have your best interests at heart!

From *Little Red Riding Hood,* told and illustrated by Elizabeth Orton Jones, 1948.

**But that doesn't mean you should give up
and crawl into your shell.**

From *I Can Fly* by Ruth Krauss, illustrated by Mary Blair, 1951.

Just hold out for someone nice!

From *The Golden Book of Little Verses* by Miriam Clark Potter, illustrated by Mary Blair, 1953.

Dating can be so glamorous. . . .

From *The Color Kittens* by Margaret Wise Brown, illustrated by Alice and Martin Provensen, 1949.

The shopping,

From *Seven Little Postmen* by Margaret Wise Brown and Edith Thacher Hurd,
illustrated by Tibor Gergely, 1952.

the courting!

From *Gaston and Josephine* by Georges Duplaix, illustrated by Feodor Rojankovsky, 1949.

The flowers,

From *Tawny Scrawny Lion* by Kathryn Jackson, illustrated by Gustaf Tenggren, 1952.

the consorting!

From "Rapunzel," *The Blue Book of Fairy Tales,* illustrated by Gordon Laite, 1959.

But sometimes the most memorable dates are the simplest ones.

From *Nursery Songs*, arranged by Leah Gale, illustrated by Corinne Malvern, 1942.

Even if you've been married forever, never stop dating each other.

From *The Little Fat Policeman* by Margaret Wise Brown and Edith Thacher Hurd, illustrated by Alice and Martin Provensen, 1950.

Love gives us a voice,

From *Nursery Songs,* arranged by Leah Gale, illustrated by Corinne Malvern, 1942.

but it needs no words.

From *My Snuggly Bunny* by Patsy Scarry, illustrated by Eloise Wilkin, 1956.

**Without love,
we wouldn't know
joy's true heights**

From *I Can Fly* by Ruth Krauss, illustrated by Mary Blair, 1951.

or the beauty in sorrow.

From *The Golden Books Treasury of Prayers from Around the World,* selected by Esther Wilkin, illustrated by Eloise Wilkin, 1975.

Love is patient and kind.

Love is sometimes . . .

From *Bow Wow! Meow! A First Book of Sounds* by Melanie Bellah,
illustrated by Trina Schart Hyman, 1963.

cake!

From *The Jolly Barnyard* by Annie North Bedford, illustrated by Tibor Gergely, 1950.

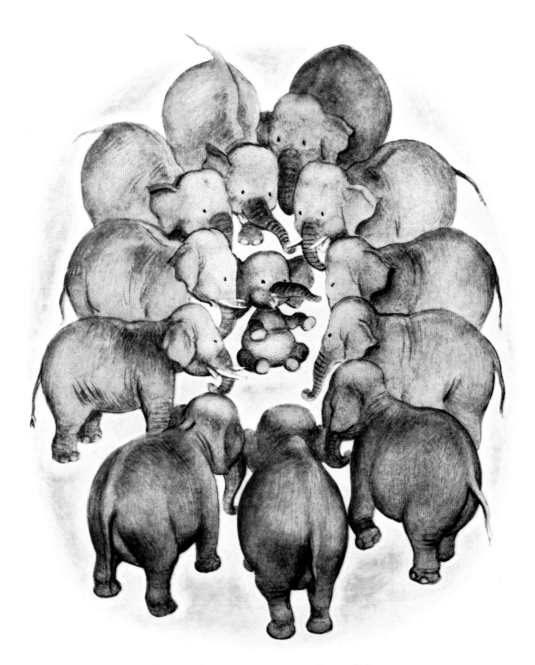

Love's got your back!

From *The Saggy Baggy Elephant* by Kathryn and Byron Jackson, illustrated by Gustaf Tenggren, 1947.

Love can be complicated

From "Beauty and the Beast," *The Blue Book of Fairy Tales,* illustrated by Gordon Laite, 1959.

or as easy as a summer breeze.

From *A Day on the Farm* by Nancy Fielding Hulick, illustrated by J. P. Miller, 1960.

Love makes you bold!

From *The Little Golden Holiday Book* by Marion Conger, illustrated by Eloise Wilkin, 1951.

Love waits,

From *My Puppy* by Patsy Scarry, illustrated by Eloise Wilkin, 1955.

and love is worth fighting for.

From *King Arthur and the Knights of the Round Table*, a Golden Illustrated Classic,
retold by Emma Gelders Sterne and Barbara Lindsay, illustrated by Gustaf Tenggren, 1962.

It leads us on flights of fancy

From *The Marvelous Merry-Go-Round* by Jane Werner,
illustrated by J. P. Miller, 1950.

or deep into a world of our own.

From "Rapunzel," *The Blue Book of Fairy Tales,* illustrated by Gordon Laite, 1959.

There is glory and grandeur in love. . . .

From *Tales from the Arabian Nights*, a Giant Golden Book,
retold by Margaret Soifer and Irwin Shapiro, illustrated by Gustaf Tenggren, 1957.

**But mostly, loves blooms
in life's day-to-day moments.**

From *The Happy Family* by Nicole, illustrated by Corinne Malvern, 1955.

It lives in our memories

From *The Little Golden Holiday Book* by Marion Conger, illustrated by Eloise Wilkin, 1951.

of simple, happy times.

From *The Bunny Book* by Patsy Scarry, illustrated by Richard Scarry, 1955.

Love brings emotions
you never dreamed you could feel.

From "A Very Big Christmas," *The Animals' Merry Christmas* by Kathryn Jackson, illustrated by Richard Scarry, 1950.

**Love reveals how strong—
and how gentle—
you can be.**

From *The New Baby* by Ruth and Harold Shane, illustrated by Eloise Wilkin, 1948.

One of the most amazing acts of love is adopting a child.

Both pages from *The Kitten Who Thought He Was a Mouse* by Miriam Norton, illustrated by Garth Williams, 1951.

'Cause there's always
room for one more!

Is there anything fiercer
than a mother's love?

From "The Three Little Kittens," *Three Bedtime Stories,* illustrated by Garth Williams, 1958.

But sometimes love is tested by your kids . . .

From *Good Little, Bad Little Girl* by Esther Wilkin, illustrated by Eloise Wilkin, 1965.

or by your spouse, especially when
you're accused of being a nag.

From *The Big Brown Bear* by Georges Duplaix, illustrated by Gustaf Tenggren, 1947.

Sometimes you feel completely in sync!

From *Circus Time* by Marion Conger, illustrated by Tibor Gergely, 1948.

Other times you wonder if you're from two different species.

From *The Golden Animal ABC*, illustrated by Garth Williams, 1954.

Sometimes a love ends—
shockingly, suddenly.

From *This World of Ours* by Jane Werner Watson, illustrated by Eloise Wilkin, 1959.

You're alone—and adrift.

From *Scuffy the Tugboat* by Gertrude Crampton, illustrated by Tibor Gergely, 1946.

A broken heart is no picnic.

From *The Saggy Baggy Elephant* by Kathryn and Byron Jackson, illustrated by Gustaf Tenggren, 1947.

It can leave you flat on your back . . .

From *Nurse Nancy* by Kathryn Jackson, illustrated by Corinne Malvern, 1952.

or feeling completely upended.

From *The Seven Sneezes* by Olga Cabral, illustrated by Tibor Gergely, 1948.

You want whatever will take away the pain.

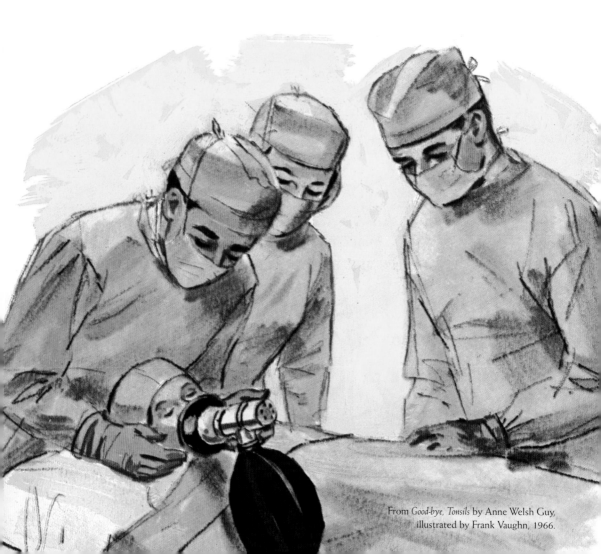

From *Good-bye, Tonsils* by Anne Welsh Guy,
illustrated by Frank Vaughn, 1966.

That's when you need those friends of yours!

From *Nurse Nancy* by Kathryn Jackson, illustrated by Corinne Malvern, 1952.

But the best medicine for heartbreak is time.

From *The Big Little Book* by Dorothy Hall Smith, illustrated by Moritz Kennel, 1962.

One day you'll find you've got your sense of adventure back!

From *Christopher and the Columbus* by Kathryn and Byron Jackson, illustrated by Tibor Gergely, 1951.

From *The Friendly Book* by Margaret Wise Brown, illustrated by Garth Williams, 1954.

Life seems quirky and fun again.

The day finally comes when you look in the mirror and see that you're ready

From *Little Red Riding Hood*,
told and illustrated by
Elizabeth Orton Jones, 1948.

to start anew.

From *Mister Dog* by Margaret Wise Brown, illustrated by Garth Williams, 1952.

You just might meet that special someone!

From *The New Golden Song Book*, arranged by Norman Lloyd, illustrated by Mary Blair, 1955.

**Next thing you know,
you're humming corny
old love songs . . .**

**'cause suddenly
they make sense!**

From *The Little Red Hen*, illustrated by J. P. Miller, 1954.

That's when it's time to put on your big-girl panties.

From *We Help Mommy* by Jean Cushman, illustrated by Eloise Wilkin, 1959.

It's time to jump in with both feet!

From *Danny Beaver's Secret* by Patsy Scarry, illustrated by Richard Scarry, 1953.

Because when it comes to love, you can't love only a little.

From *The Friendly Book* by Margaret Wise Brown, illustrated by Garth Williams, 1954.

Love lavishly!

From *The Twelve Dancing Princesses* by the Brothers Grimm, retold by Jane Werner, illustrated by Sheilah Beckett, 1954.

Be ready to play the hero . . .

From *King Arthur and the Knights of the Round Table,* a Golden Illustrated Classic,
retold by Emma Gelders Sterne and Barbara Lindsay, illustrated by Gustaf Tenggren, 1962.

and the fool.

Believe that the magical moment will come

From *The Wild Swans* by Hans Christian Andersen, illustrated by Gordon Laite, 1970, 2014.

when "I" becomes "we."

From *The House That Jack Built*, illustrated by J. P. Miller, 1954.

From *Home for a Bunny* by Margaret Wise Brown, illustrated by Garth Williams, 1956.

**Be ready
to take a chance . . .**

on love.

From *Home for a Bunny* by Margaret Wise Brown, illustrated by Garth Williams, 1956.